THE LITTLE BOOK OF

FROZEN
DRINKS

And Other Party Classics

VIRGINIA REYNOLDS

ILLUSTRATED BY KERREN BARBAS

PETER PAUPER PRESS, INC.
WHITE PLAINS, NEW YORK

For the Taconics,
who need no excuse to party

SPECIAL THANKS TO:

LA BUENA VIDA RESTAURANT, AKUMAL
DADY'O, CANCUN
CHEF CHRIS HOWERTON, LOUISVILLE
JOE'S STONE CRAB, SOUTH BEACH, MIAMI
ANDREW ORTH, THE COURT OF TWO SISTERS, NEW ORLEANS
PURE NIGHTCLUB, LAS VEGAS
RED SQUARE, LAS VEGAS
THE ROSE BAR, SOUTH BEACH, MIAMI
BROOK SARGEANT, WATER BAR, SYDNEY
TERRANEO BAR, RIO DE JANEIRO
ALISTAIR WILSON, PLANET CHAMPAGNE BAR, CAPE TOWN
SUZANNE ZENKEL, NEW YORK

Designed by Heather Zschock
Illustrations copyright © 2007 Kerren Barbas

Copyright © 2007
Peter Pauper Press, Inc.
202 Mamaroneck Avenue
White Plains, NY 10601
All rights reserved
ISBN 978-1-59359-861-7
Printed in Hong Kong
7 6 5 4 3 2 1

Visit us at www.peterpauper.com

THE LITTLE
PINK BOOK OF
FROZEN
DRINKS

CONTENTS

how to party like it's 1999

THROW A BASH THEY'LL NEVER FORGET

I'm ombibulous.
I drink every known alcoholic
drink and enjoy them all.

H.L. MENCKEN

Break out the blender and the bongo drums—it's party time! From the trendiest urban sophisticate to the straight-ahead free spirit whose idea of accessorizing is donning a lampshade, just about everyone loves to party. Who needs a reason? Let's celebrate!

Nothing gets a party going like good company (you'll supply that) and some swanky, snazzy party drinks. We've collected recipes from four corners of the globe for your special bash—the one they'll be talking about for years to come.

Discover the secrets for creating splashy tiki

treasures, chic signature drinks, and crowd-pleasing party standbys. Wow your guests with retro fruit concoctions served in pineapple shells, or go sleek with the latest 'tinis from the world's hottest nightspots. Just crank up the icemaker and get behind the bar. We'll supply the know-how. You supply the fun!

Party on!

THE RIGHT STUFF

Anyone can throw a party, even a good party. But if you want your soiree to be the stuff of legend, you may need to acquire a few specialty accoutrements. In addition to the usual items found behind the home bar—jiggers, shakers, spoons, and strainers—you'll need:

Hardware

- Your **blender** is your best friend, especially when whipping up frozen goodies. If you plan to make more than one type of drink, ask friends to lend their blenders, or you'll spend the party in the kitchen rinsing out yours between rounds. Rule: one blender per type of cocktail.

- The truly dedicated (or those who have viewed too many reruns of *Home Improvement*) may purchase a gasoline-powered blender for use at the beach or on camping trips. So, ladies, the next time your man makes a crack about "girly drinks," send him here: www.gasblender.com. He'll be whipping up banana daiquiris in no time.

- Frozen drink machine. Think you'll make a habit of frozen drinks? Then this is a worthwhile investment. They come in various sizes and price ranges, and many double as smoothie-makers—ideal for throwing together a morning-after hangover helper.

- **Melon baller.** The smaller, the better. If you're planning melon-flavored cocktails or want to use melon as a garnish, make your melon balls early in the day (and thread them on skewers, if needed). A quick trip to the freezer won't hurt them, and it will keep them cold in and on your guests' drinks.

- **Muddler.** You can't do mojitos or juleps without one of these blunt instruments to infuse the fruit flavors.

- **Ice.** Frozen drinks use up ice quickly. Begin making ice cubes several days before your event, storing them in zip-top freezer bags. If your icemaker can't keep up, purchase several bags of commercially packaged ice.

- **Large glasses.** Visit tag sales for outrageous parfait and goblet-style glasses. Invest in a set of tiki mugs for your next luau.

- **Swizzle sticks.** Collect a whole set! Nothing says "let's party" like kitschy swizzle sticks shaped like flamingos, palm trees, or U.S. states. Other fun accessories include paper parasols, light-up or other novelty reusable "ice" cubes, and themed drink accessories (we've seen monkeys, dolphins, and mermaids). They're available at your favorite party shop.

Software

- **Simple syrup.** Many bartenders prefer simple syrup to sugar in sweetened cocktails because it blends easily and provides a smooth taste. Trust the pros on this one. To make your own: Dissolve 1 pound  granulated sugar in 8 ounces warm water. Stirring continually, add an additional 8 ounces of water until sugar is completely dissolved. Store syrup in the refrigerator, in a jar with a tight-fitting lid.

- **Monin.** This French product is well worth the investment if you plan on dabbling in exotic flavors. The Monin Company (www.monin.com) produces naturally flavored—and highly concentrated—syrups in over 80 flavors, including guava, pistachio, even pomegranate. There's no limit to what you can create, and the syrups can also be used to flavor coffees, teas, and other beverages. Monin is also available at fine grocery stores.

- **Specialty ingredients.** Before mixing, review recipes and ensure you have sufficient quantities of ingredients on hand, especially the more exotic items. For many of these, there are no substitutes. And remember, if you take the trouble to purchase authentic ingredients, your guests will sing your praises as a bon vivant and all-around cool cat (or kitten).

- **Colored sugars.** These sugars are available commercially in craft, gourmet food, and specialty kitchenware stores. Or, you can make your own using granulated sugar (about 1/4 cup) and a tiny drop of food coloring. Stir together and store in a closed container until needed.

- **Flavored sugars for rimming glasses.** The most popular of these is vanilla. To make **vanilla sugar**, add a whole vanilla bean to about 2 cups of granulated sugar. Cover and store for about 2 weeks. The longer you leave the vanilla bean in the sugar, the more pronounced the vanilla flavor will be. Experiment with other flavors:

  - **Lemon sugar.** To 1 cup granulated sugar, add the finely chopped zest of 3 lemons. Pulse briefly in the food processor to combine and break down any remaining large pieces of zest. Add another 1 cup of sugar, mix well, and spread onto greaseproof paper to dry out. Store in a closed container.

- **Rose petal sugar** will add a delicate floral flavor to your cocktails. Using a mortar and pestle, pound 2 cups of fresh rose petals (make sure they're pesticide- and blemish-free!) with 1 cup of granulated sugar. After 1 week, sift out rose petals, if desired.

- **Create your own sugar flavor** with a drop of your favorite Monin syrup.

- Add food coloring and flavoring as described above to create **sugars that are both colored** *and* **flavored**.

let's get ready to rum-ba!

COOL DELIGHTS FOR TROPICAL NIGHTS

Ginger: *Wahine wiki huki luki nu, and
I mean that from the bottom of my heart.*
Gilligan: *That's beautiful. What's it mean?*
Ginger: *It means this bar is off-limits
to all military personnel.*

"GILLIGAN'S ISLAND" (1964)

From Aruba to Zanzibar, you'll find concoctions that capture the essence of every exotic locale. (And chances are someone has been there before you and brought back the souvenir cocktail glass to prove it.)

To enhance your drinking pleasure, we'd like to share a point or two regarding the total tropical experience—ideally, an escape in a glass. If you close your eyes, you should hear the relaxing rhythms of steel drums. Hence:

- Garnish is everything! Experiment with exotic fruits, with and without skins. (How about those spiky Asian lychees? Or a sliced star fruit?) And don't forget the little paper umbrellas!

- Many of these drinks are strong, but, if properly prepared, they will be neither overpowering nor cloying. They will taste sweet and smooth, without any alcoholic sharpness or bite.

A LOTTA COLADAS

What's your idea of a sun-splashed idyll? A thatched hut on a deserted beach? A palm-shaded colonial estate in the tropics? Maybe a swashbuckling pirate ship on the high seas? Whatever your style, there's a creamy, slushy, colada cooler to complement it!

"Colada" is actually Spanish for "strained." In addition to the famous Piña Colada—the official beverage of Puerto Rico—any sweet, rum-based cocktail blended with crushed ice can claim to be a colada.

Here's the original recipe, as mixed by a mysterious bartender known only as "Monchito" in Old San Juan one hot night in 1954.

CLASSIC PIÑA COLADA

1-1/2 oz. golden rum
1-1/2 oz. coconut cream
4 oz. pineapple juice
About 1 cup ice cubes

Blend all ingredients in blender until slushy.
Pour into a chilled parfait glass or half
coconut shell and garnish with pineapple
chunks and a cherry. You'll soon be livin'
la vida loca.

Some people say that the classic can't be improved upon. But if you feel like trying, we offer a few scrumptious variations:

BANANA COLADA

1-1/2 oz. dark rum
2 oz. coconut cream
2 oz. pineapple juice
1 medium ripe banana, divided in half
6–7 ice cubes

Blend all ingredients in blender until slushy. Pour into a chilled parfait glass. **Tip:** As banana tends to overpower the other flavors in this drink, begin by using just half the banana. Add more as desired.

The editors are not responsible for any monkey business occurring after consumption of this drink.

CAPTAIN'S COLADA OR BUMBOO

Substitute Captain Morgan or other spiced rum for the golden rum in the classic recipe on page 19. Hoist the Jolly Roger!

Captain Jack Sparrow: *There now, drink up. Finest bumboo in the whole Caribbean.*

PIRATES OF THE CARIBBEAN: THE CURSE OF THE BLACK PEARL (2003)

(Bumboo is a drink made from rum, sugar, and spices, and favored by pirates. Arrrr!)

KEY LIME COLADA

1-1/2 oz. lemon-flavored rum
1/2 oz. KeKe Beach key lime-flavored liqueur
1-1/2 oz. fresh lime juice
1 oz. coconut cream
About 1 cup ice cubes

Blend all ingredients in blender until slushy. Pour into a chilled parfait glass. Decorate with a generous wedge of key lime and shavings of sweetened coconut.

KIWI COLADA

1-1/2 oz. light rum
1-1/2 oz. melon-flavored liqueur
3 oz. pineapple juice
2 oz. coconut cream
1 oz. whipping cream
2 kiwis, peeled and roughly chopped (remove seeds if desired)
About 1 cup ice cubes

Blend all ingredients in blender until slushy.

Pour into a chilled parfait glass. Garnish with a skewer of fresh fruits: melon, pineapple, kiwi chunks.

MOCHA COLADA
It's a tropical jolt of java!

1-1/2 oz. light rum
1/2 oz. coffee liqueur
2 oz. cold espresso or strong coffee
1 oz. coconut cream
1 tsp. chocolate syrup
About 1 cup ice cubes

Blend all ingredients in blender until slushy. Pour into chilled parfait glass. Artfully place a few chocolate-covered espresso beans on top.

SKINNY PIÑA COLADA
Luscious flavor, lower in calories.

1-1/2 oz. coconut-flavored rum
1 oz. pineapple juice
2 Tbs. low-carb vanilla yogurt
6–7 ice cubes

Blend all ingredients in blender until slushy. Pour into chilled parfait glass. Embellish with fresh coconut shavings. (Approximately 78 calories.)

STRAWBERRY COLADA

3/4 oz. dark rum
3/4 oz. light rum
4 oz. pineapple juice
1 oz. coconut cream
4 strawberries, hulled
About 1 cup ice cubes

Blend all ingredients in blender until slushy. Pour into a chilled parfait glass. Garnish with one perfect strawberry.

CREATE YOUR OWN COLADAS WITH SEASONAL FRUITS AND BERRIES. **Tip:** Use caution with frozen berries, as they tend to add extra sweetness to the drink. They also blend faster—add them last, when the mixture is almost slushy.

BEYOND THE COLADA

The drinks that follow all feature rum; they're fruity, exotic, and they perfectly capture the laid-back spirit of tropical life.

BAHAMA MAMA

You may want to make every day "Mama's Day" after a couple of these coconut-laced concoctions.

1/2 oz. 151-proof rum
1/2 oz. coconut rum or coconut liqueur
1/2 oz. dark rum
1/2 oz. coffee liqueur
4 oz. pineapple juice
Juice of 1/2 lemon

TRADITIONAL METHOD:

Mix ingredients in a cocktail shaker with cracked ice. Strain into an iced highball glass. Garnish with fresh fruit.

Combine ingredients with about 1-1/2 cups ice cubes in a blender. Blend until slushy. Pour into chilled Collins glasses. (This method makes enough for two.)

BEACHCOMBER

After combing "Gilligan's Island" for treasures, kick back with Thurston and Lovey Howell—they never missed a prime-time cocktail hour!

1-1/2 oz. light rum
1/2 oz. Cointreau
1/2 oz. fresh lime juice
2 dashes maraschino liqueur or grenadine
1 cup crushed ice

Mix all ingredients with crushed ice in blender or mixer. Be careful not to over-mix, or mixture will become watery. Pour (don't strain) into an oversized wine goblet and garnish with an ostentatious lime wheel.

FROZEN RUM RUNNER

Rum runners—spirits smugglers—flourished during Prohibition, when Al Capone, among others, kept American speakeasies supplied with liquor, even as he threw non-stop parties at sea on luxury yachts near the "Rum Row" ships anchored just outside U.S. jurisdiction.

1 oz. light rum
1/4 oz. 151-proof rum (optional)
1/2 oz. banana liqueur
1/2 oz. blackberry brandy
1/2 oz. grenadine
1/4 oz. Rose's Lime Juice
Splash sweet-and-sour mix
Splash pineapple juice
About 1 cup ice cubes

Blend all ingredients in blender until slushy. Pour into a chilled parfait glass. If desired, pour 151-proof rum on top. Garnish with a slice of lime and maraschino cherry. For a true "speakeasy" experience, serve in teacups!

Philip Marlowe: *In the old days . . . he used to run rum out of Mexico and I was on the other side. We used to swap shots between drinks, or drinks between shots, whichever you like.*

THE BIG SLEEP (1946)

HURRICANE

This famous Bourbon Street staple was created during WWII, when whiskey and other spirits were rare, and rum readily available. Reportedly invented in the 1940s in Pat O'Brien's fabled French Quarter Bar, the Hurricane was originally served in a hurricane lamp; today's hosts should serve them in the glass of the same name.

1-1/2 oz. dark rum
1-1/2 oz. light rum
1 oz. fresh lime juice
1 oz. orange juice
1/4 cup passion fruit juice or 1 Tbs. passion fruit syrup
1 tsp. superfine sugar
1 tsp. grenadine

TRADITIONAL METHOD:

To dissolve sugar, this drink requires some "Category 5" agitation in a cocktail shaker.

Combine all ingredients except grenadine until sugar dissolves. Add cracked ice and grenadine and shake some more. Strain into an iced hurricane glass. Garnish with cherries and orange slices.

FROZEN METHOD:

Blend all ingredients except grenadine in a blender for 15 seconds, or until sugar dissolves. Add about 1 cup ice cubes and grenadine and blend until slushy. Garnish as above.

Ralphie: *Hey Curly, what all happens in a hurricane?*

Curly: *The wind blows so hard the ocean gets up on its hind legs and walks right across the land.*

KEY LARGO, 1948

MISSIONARY'S DOWNFALL

Poor missionaries never stood a chance once they'd sampled the local fare. Oddly, none wrote home to complain.

1 oz. light rum
1/2 oz. peach brandy
1-1/2 oz. fresh lime juice
1/4 oz. simple syrup
1/2 slice fresh pineapple
About 25 fresh mint leaves (or the leaves from
    4–5 sprigs of fresh mint)
About 1 cup ice cubes

Blend all ingredients in blender until smooth. Pour into a chilled highball glass or large goblet. Garnish with pineapple and mint.

international party hot spot

Louis: *In the spring of 1988,
I returned to New Orleans, and
as soon as I smelled the air, I knew
I was home. It was rich, almost
sweet, like the scent of jasmine
and roses around our old courtyard.
I walked the streets, savoring
that long lost perfume.*

INTERVIEW WITH THE VAMPIRE:
THE VAMPIRE CHRONICLES (1994)

The home of Sazerac, Southern
Comfort, and (allegedly) even the
word "cocktail," New Orleans practi-
cally invented the party! (Although
anyone who's been to Mardi Gras

knows Fat Tuesday is no mere party.) Welcome to the Big Easy, and to The Court of Two Sisters, a 200-year-old French Quarter landmark. This sophisticated restaurant, the former home of a pair of celebrated Creole sisters, is known for its fine dining and libations. Relax in the wisteria-shaded courtyard and sample its bestselling Bayou Bash. Or try the award-winning Crescent City Cooler. You'll be charmed by genteel service and New Orleans jazz.

Laissez les bon temps rouler!

(Cajun for "Let the good times roll!")

BAYOU BASH

1-1/4 oz. Southern Comfort
1-1/4 oz. sweet-and-sour mix
1 oz. orange juice
3/4 oz. cherry juice
3/4 oz. pineapple juice
3/4 oz. red wine
1/4 oz. grenadine

Shake all ingredients except wine with cracked ice. Strain into a hurricane glass. Top with red wine. Garnish with a "flag" (barspeak for a skewer with an orange slice and a cherry).

CRESCENT CITY COOLER

Second-place winner, 2006 "Classic Rum Cocktails with a Twist" competition, sponsored by Bacardi Superior Rum and *Culinary Concierge* magazine.

2 oz. Bacardi light rum
10 fresh mint leaves, cleaned
Dash simple syrup
2 dashes Angostura bitters
2 dashes Peychaud's bitters
Juice of 2 lime wedges
2 oz. ginger ale
3/4 oz. cranberry juice

Place mint leaves into a Collins glass. Add the syrup and both bitters. Muddle for 10 seconds. Add lime juice, rum, and ginger ale. Fill glass with ice and stir. Top with cranberry juice. Garnish with lime wheel and a fresh mint sprig.

TWO SISTERS TODDY

1/2 oz. Grand Marnier
1/2 oz. Maker's Mark bourbon
1/2 oz. strawberry liqueur

Stir with cracked ice and strain into a chilled cocktail glass. Garnish with a lemon twist. *Reproduced by kind permission of The Court of Two Sisters (www.courtoftwosisters.com).*

PARTY CLASSIC: MAI TAI

The story of the Mai Tai—and that of its creator, Victor "Trader Vic" Bergeron—has it all: the allure of the South Seas, travelers from afar, and a rags-to-riches story. A self-starter with a colorful personality, Vic opened his first restaurant, Hinky Dinks, in Oakland, California, in 1932. By 1936, the name had changed to the eponymous "Trader Vic's." The Mai Tai was born in 1944 when Vic served a new drink creation to visiting Tahitian friends. One of them took a sip and exclaimed, *"Mai tai—roa ae!"* That's Polynesian for "Out of this world—the best!" Today, there are 25 Trader Vic restaurants worldwide.

Trader Vic's intrigues everyone. You think of beaches and moonlight and pretty girls. It is complete escape.

"TRADER VIC" BERGERON

Although potent, the flavors in the Mai Tai are subtle: no showy pineapple or coconut here. Instead, Vic wanted to spotlight the drink's fine rums and liqueurs. While the original specialty ingredients favored by the Trader are hard to find, follow his lead in seeking top-quality dark Jamaican rums (the older, the better) and orgeat and rock-candy syrups. Pre-packaged Mai Tai mix is available, but it's more fun to try to replicate the original recipe. We include it here for purists.

THE ORIGINAL MAI TAI

Ever the perfectionist, Vic always specified the brands to be used in his creations.

2 oz. 17-year-old Wray & Nephew Jamaican rum
1/2 oz. DeKuyper Orange Curaçao
*1/2 oz. French Garnier Orgeat**
1/4 oz. rock candy syrup
Juice of 1 lime (reserve fruit)

Shake all ingredients in a cocktail shaker with cracked ice. Drop half the lime shell into the bottom of a highball glass and fill with ice. Strain the drink into the prepared glass and garnish with a generous sprig of fresh mint. Perfect!

If the original is a bit overwhelming, try a later version. (The Mai Tai underwent several revisions over time as specialty rums became scarce.)

Easy Mai Tai

2 oz. dark rum
1/2 oz. curaçao
*1/2 oz. orgeat**
1/4 oz. rock candy syrup or simple syrup
Juice of 1 lime

Prepare as above. If you want to simplify even more, substitute 4 oz. of packaged Mai Tai mix for the last four ingredients.

*ORGEAT (pronounced "or-zat") is a flavored syrup made from sugar, orange flower water, and almonds. It has a distinctive almond flavor, but don't consider substituting regular almond syrup for the real thing; it doesn't quite measure up. Conveniently, orgeat is available at www.tradervics.com.

PARTY CLASSIC: ZOMBIE

Before *Night of the Living Dead*, there was the Zombie. The drink's creator, the legendary Donn Beach of tiki fame, would permit patrons to consume only two of these potent concoctions apiece in his Don the Beachcomber restaurants. We've included the basic recipe for the original killer drink, as well as a slightly less complicated—and less intoxicating—version.

ORIGINAL ZOMBIE

1-1/4 oz. spiced rum
1 oz. 151-proof rum
1 oz. dark rum
1 oz. golden rum
1 oz. white rum
3/4 oz. Heering Cherry Liqueur
1 oz. fresh grapefruit juice
3/4 oz. fresh lime juice
1/2 oz. falernum*

1/2 oz. simple syrup
3 dashes grenadine
2 dashes Pernod or other anise-flavored
  liqueur
1/2 cup water

If you can find a large enough shaker, shake all ingredients with cracked ice and strain into highball or hurricane glasses filled with crushed ice. Garnish with lime and cherry.

Serves two or three, depending on size of glass. If your cocktail shaker won't hold it all, whirl ingredients briefly in a blender before transferring in batches to a cocktail shaker with cracked ice.

*FALERNUM is a non-alcoholic syrup flavored with almond, ginger, lime, and sometimes vanilla and allspice. Don't confuse it with the alcoholic liqueur of the same name.

ZOMBIE FOR DUMMIES (ZUMMIE)

1 oz. dark rum
1 oz. golden rum
1 oz. light rum
1/2 oz. 151-proof rum
1 oz. apricot brandy
1 oz. papaya or passion fruit juice
1 oz. pineapple juice
Juice of 1 lime

Mix all ingredients except 151-proof rum in a cocktail shaker with cracked ice and strain into an iced highball or parfait glass. Float 151-proof rum on top and garnish with a mint sprig dusted with powdered sugar.

Radio Announcer: *Eyewitnesses say they are ordinary-looking people. Some say they appear to be in a kind of trance. Others describe them as being misshapen monsters. At this point, there's no really authentic way for us to say who or what to look for and guard yourself against.*

NIGHT OF THE LIVING DEAD (1968)

run out of rum?

ISLAND MANGO SLUSH

This exotic cocktail has it all: sweet mango, spicy ginger, the lush vanilla and oak notes of fine bourbon, and a refreshing cap of mint. The Island Mango Slush won the Grand Prize at the 2005 Kentucky Bourbon Festival and was deemed official Festival drink of 2006. Already famous in Louisville and Bardstown, Kentucky, it deserves a wider reputation.

9 oz. W.L. Weller 12-year-old bourbon whiskey

4 oz. ginger ale

3 whole mangoes, peeled and diced, plus 1 extra for garnish

1 Tbs. fresh ginger, peeled and diced

1 Tbs. sugar
4 cups ice cubes
Leaves from 1 sprig of fresh mint
Additional mint sprigs to garnish

Moisten the rims of 4 chilled cocktail glasses with a little cut mango and spin glass rims in sugar. Blend all ingredients except reserved mango and mint sprigs in a blender until slushy. Pour into prepared glasses. Garnish with thin, elegant slices of mango and a sprig of fresh mint. *Reproduced by kind permission of Chef Chris Howerton of Louisville, the drink's creator.*

Bourbon does for me what the piece of cake did for Proust.

WALKER PERCY

frosty fiesta

FAVORITES FROM SOUTH OF THE BORDER

Buscemi: *The stranger shot him,*
walked over to the bartender, paid, and left.
Short bartender: *So the bartender lived?*
The bartender never gets killed!

DESPERADO (1995)

S outh of the border, they know how to party! And the unique climates of the Caribbean, Mexico, and South America make these regions conducive wellsprings for tropical delights of all kinds.

Sugar cane, cultivated throughout Latin America, is the basis for rum and cachaça (pronounced ka-sha-sa). Citrus and tropical fruits abound. Finally, succulent blue agave, which thrives in Mexico, brings its distinctive piquant flavor to the party. All these ingredients combine endlessly and deliciously in many cocktails, both traditional and contemporary.

This is an official "thank you"—to Mexico, for the margarita; to Cuba, for daiquiris and mojitos; and to Brazil, for the caipirinha family of cocktails.

DAIQUIRIS

Rum. Lime juice. A little sugar. Short and simple, like a line from a Hemingway novel. Although nothing could be more straightforward, these compatible elements are the building blocks of many an exotic quencher. There's probably no fruit that hasn't been tried in a daiquiri recipe—tamarind daiquiri, anyone?

Created in Cuba early in the 20th century, the daiquiri earned renown in the celebrated Havana watering hole, El Floridita, a favorite of Ernest Hemingway's. For a true literary experience, drop in and order a *"Papa Doble,"* the writer's favorite double daiquiri, or another drink specialty, and let the atmosphere take you back in time.

Note: In their pure form, daiquiris are intended to be sharp, tart drinks. Some of the fruity variations will soften this tartness somewhat, but it's important to use white—not golden—rum in a daiquiri cocktail for the proper bite.

He had drunk double frozen daiquiris, the great ones that Constante made, that had no taste of alcohol and felt, as you drank them, the way downhill glacier skiing feels running through powder snow. . . .

ERNEST HEMINGWAY,
ISLANDS IN THE STREAM

BASIC DAIQUIRI

2 oz. light rum

1 oz. fresh lime juice, strained of pulp (Please don't insult us by using the bottled variety.)

1/2 oz. simple syrup or 1 tsp. superfine sugar

Shake well with cracked ice and strain into a chilled cocktail glass. For the tart and tangy, garnish with a slice of lime; for the softly sweet, a maraschino cherry will do. May also be served on the rocks in an old-fashioned glass.

TO MAKE FROZEN:

Because the drink will be diluted by ice, you can add a little more rum, lime juice, and sugar. Blend with about 1 cup ice cubes and pour into a chilled goblet rimmed with sugar.

BANANA DAIQUIRI

1-1/2 oz. light rum
1 Tbs. triple sec
1-1/2 oz. fresh lime juice
1 tsp. superfine sugar
1 whole ripe banana, peeled and broken into
*   chunks*
About 1 cup ice cubes

Blend rum, triple sec, lime juice, sugar, and ice at high speed until slushy. Add banana and blend until smooth. Pour into a chilled goblet and decorate with a banana wedge and a cherry. Now don a pair of reflective sunglasses and make like the *generalissimo* of a banana republic.

CREOLE DAIQUIRI

A specialty of Martinique, this is best prepared with this Caribbean island's own Rhum Clément. Kind of a rum-cachaça hybrid, Rhum Clément is distilled from the juice of sugar cane, and is the base for Creole Shrubb, an orange-flavored liqueur similar to curaçao (which may be substituted).

2 oz. light rum or Rhum Clément
1 oz. Clément Creole Shrubb
2 oz. fresh lime juice

Shake well with cracked ice and strain into a chilled cocktail glass. Serve with a lime slice.

TO MAKE FROZEN:

Blend all ingredients with about 1 cup ice cubes until slushy and pour into a chilled goblet. Garnish with lime.

FLORIDITA (HEMINGWAY'S) DAIQUIRI

Looking for literary inspiration? Follow in the footsteps of "Papa" Hemingway, for whom this tangy citrus quencher is named.

2 oz. light rum
1/4 oz. maraschino liqueur
1 oz. fresh lime juice
1/4 oz. fresh grapefruit juice
1/2 tsp. superfine sugar

Shake all ingredients vigorously with cracked ice and strain into a chilled cocktail glass. Although Hemingway would probably have eschewed garnish, you can add a maraschino cherry or thin lime slice. You're ready to write the Great American Novel, or join a Lost Generation.

Double the ingredients and you've got your own *"Papa Doble."*

PEACH DAIQUIRI

1-1/2 oz. light rum
1 oz. fresh lime juice
1 tsp. superfine sugar
1/2 fresh peach, peeled and sliced
Splash of triple sec
About 1 cup ice cubes

Blend all ingredients at medium speed until slushy. Pour into a chilled parfait glass. For a sunset glow, add a few drops of grenadine. Garnish with a fresh peach slice. Now that's peachy!

Eddie: *Drinking don't bother my memory. If it did I wouldn't drink. I couldn't. You see, I'd forget how good it was, then where'd I be? Start drinkin' water, again.*

To Have and Have Not (1944)

SMOOTH PINEAPPLE DAIQUIRI

If you're lucky enough to find those cute little mini-pineapples in your local market, snap them up and fill them with this super-smooth concoction.

1-1/2 oz. light rum
1 Tbs. fresh lime juice
1/2 tsp. superfine sugar
4 pineapple chunks, about 1/2 cup (we recommend fresh, but canned will do in an emergency)
About 1 cup ice cubes

 Blend at high speed until smooth and pour into your choice of exotic vessel. Serve to each guest with a paper lei and crank up the hula music. This would be a good time to demonstrate your prowess on the ukulele.

MARGARITAS

It's hard to beat a good margarita—made with premium tequila, fresh lime juice, and kosher salt. It's like a little black dress—perfect on its own, spectacular when paired with the right accessories. Stories abound regarding the margarita's origins, but most agree that it was born south of the border. We especially like the tale that links the drink to actress Rita Hayworth, whose real name was Margarita.

It's a testament to this cocktail's versatility that it has inspired dozens of variations and its own signature drinking glass: the saucer-shaped margarita glass.

 A word on packaged margarita mixes: although we always recommend you use fresh ingredients (especially when making individual cocktails), mixes

have advantages if preparing quantities of drinks for large groups. Nobody has to spend hours squeezing citrus fruits, and the mixes are easy to use and store. Just follow the directions, and store unused portions after the party (many come in handy "buckets").

BASIC MARGARITA

Sometimes you just have to get back to basics. In the ideal margarita, the sourness of the lime is offset by the sweet notes of the triple sec, and salt complements tequila's unique flavor. It's the perfect "trifecta"—a salty-sweet-sour mixture.

1-1/2 oz. tequila
1/2 oz. triple sec
Juice of 1/2 fresh lime
Kosher or sea salt

Moisten the rim of a chilled margarita glass

with a piece of cut lime and spin glass rim in salt. Don't overcoat; the drinker should be able to taste the tequila through the salt. Mix all ingredients in a cocktail shaker with cracked ice. Strain into salted glass and garnish with a lime wedge.

Note: Cointreau may be substituted for triple sec, but the result will be slightly sweeter.

TO MAKE FROZEN:

Combine all ingredients (except salt) with about 1 cup ice cubes and blend until slushy. Pour into prepared glass.

COSMOLITO

If Carrie Bradshaw was vacationing in Cancun, this is what she'd order: a hybrid of her signature cosmopolitan and the classic margarita.

1-1/2 oz. silver tequila
3/4 oz. triple sec
2 oz. cranberry juice
Juice of 1/2 lime
Pink sugar or salt

Moisten rim of a chilled margarita glass with cut lime and spin glass in sugar or salt to coat rim. Shake all ingredients well with cracked ice and strain into prepared glass. Balance a little slice of lime on the rim of the glass, as if it's tottering in high-heeled shoes.

GINGERITA

The secret of this drink is grated fresh ginger for tongue-tickling tang.

1 oz. tequila
1 oz. Grand Marnier
1 oz. fresh lime juice
1 tsp. freshly grated ginger
1 tsp. simple syrup
Kosher or sea salt

Moisten the rim of a chilled margarita glass with a piece of cut lime and spin glass rim in salt. Fill prepared glass with crushed ice. Shake remaining ingredients with cracked ice and strain over crushed ice. Garnish with a lime slice.

MANGO MARGARITA

What is it about mangoes that makes them so perfect in frozen and party drinks? Is it their exotic sweetness? Their easy blendability? We don't care—we love mangoes!

1-1/2 oz. tequila
1/2 oz. Cointreau
1/2 oz. fresh lemon juice
1/2 oz. fresh lime juice
Few dashes mango-flavored Monin (see page 13)
1/2 fresh mango, peeled and sliced
About 1 cup ice cubes
Vanilla sugar (see page 14)

Moisten the rim of a chilled margarita glass with mango-flavored Monin syrup, and spin rim in vanilla sugar. Blend remaining ingredients until slushy. Pour into prepared glass. Decorate with a mango slice as wide as an African sunset. *Reproduced by kind permission of Planet Champagne Bar, Cape Town (see page 110).*

PASSION MARGARITA

3/4 oz. tequila
3/4 oz. Alizé Passion fruit liqueur
1/2 oz. Cointreau
3/4 oz. fresh lime juice
Kosher or sea salt

Moisten rim of a chilled margarita glass with
cut lime and spin glass in sugar to coat rim.
Shake all ingredients well with cracked ice
and strain into prepared glass. Serve naked,
with a single orchid flower next to (not in)
the glass.

PATRIOTIC MARGARITA

Uncle Sam wants YOU to try one of these!

1 oz. silver tequila
1 oz. Hpnotiq liqueur (a blue-tinted blend of vodka, cognac, and tropical fruit juices)
1 oz. coconut milk
1 oz. fresh lime juice
1 oz. pineapple juice
1 oz. sweetened strawberry puree (see below)
About 1 cup ice cubes
Shredded sweetened coconut

TO PUREE STRAWBERRIES:

Blend 4–5 frozen strawberries with 1 tsp. sugar. Set aside.

Moisten the rim of a chilled margarita glass with Hpnotiq liqueur. Spin glass in shredded coconut. Pour Hpnotiq liqueur into prepared glass. Blend tequila, coconut milk, lime juice, pineapple juice, and ice in blender until slushy. Pour 1/2 of blended mixture over Hpnotiq carefully, so that it does not mix with the liqueur. Blend remaining mixture with strawberry puree and layer on top. Garnish with an all-American strawberry and a little paper flag. Now sit back and watch the fireworks.

SAKE MARGARITA

East meets west in this new twist on the classic. Sake, a rice wine from Japan, stands up surprisingly well to the salt-and-lime treatment. Try serving in pottery cups or bowls on a tray decorated with paper fans.

2 oz. sake
1/2 oz. Cointreau
1-1/2 oz. lime juice
About 1 cup ice cubes
Kosher or sea salt

Moisten the rim of your choice of glassware with a cut lime and spin glass in salt to coat rim. Blend ingredients until slushy and pour into prepared glass.

WHITE COCORITA

1 oz. silver tequila
1/2 oz. coconut rum
2 oz. cream of coconut
1 oz. fresh lime juice

Shake all ingredients with cracked ice and strain into half a coconut shell. Decorate with a paper umbrella and two straws.

Now tequila may be the favored beverage of outlaws, but that doesn't mean it gives them preferential treatment.

TOM ROBBINS

all tequila is not created equal

Tequila is Mexico. It's the only product that identifies us as a culture.

CARMELITA ROMAN

Don't even *think* of calling it "cactus juice." Tequila is a liquor distilled from the sap of the blue agave plant—a succulent that flourishes in the red volcanic soil of the Mexican state of Jalisco, between the Tequila Volcano and the Rio Grande River Valley. Mexico's amazing blue agave growing region has even been declared a World Heritage site by UNESCO. By law, tequila for export must contain at least 51 percent blue agave.

THE VARIETIES OF TEQUILA:

Silver (blanco) is bottled immediately after distillation. Clear in color, it usually has a higher alcoholic content and a distinctive agave taste.

Gold (oro) contains added color and flavors—usually caramel. Its mellower, sweeter flavor makes it ideal for use in many fruit-flavored margaritas.

Reposado is aged in oak for up to one year. The flavor softens naturally but still retains the characteristic taste of blue agave.

Añejo spends longer than a year in oak casks. The wood imparts its own color and flavor to the tequila, creating a unique bouquet and taste dear to the palates of tequila lovers.

Reserva is Spanish for "get your wallet out." After eight years in oak barrels, this rare liquor is often snapped up by collectors.

Yes, but what about the worm? Sorry, kids. Mexican-bottled tequila doesn't come with a snack in the bottle. American-bottled tequila and some types of mezcal (another spirit distilled from other varieties of agave plant) may include a butterfly caterpillar, which is perfectly safe to eat, but—sorry again—contains no aphrodisiac or hallucinogenic properties.

MOJITOS

Although technically a Cuban import, the mojito is actually cousin to an old American standby, the mint julep: both are muddled infusions that include fresh mint and sugar. The similarity ends there, however. The mojito had a long history in the cane fields of Cuba and Havana hot spots before migrating into the glasses of today's tipplers.

Mojitos marry the sweetness of rum and sugar cane juice with the tartness of lime, the cool aromatics of fresh mint leaves, and a touch of effervescence. To properly prepare a

 mojito, you must master the skill of muddling—mashing together fruit, leaves, and a little liquid in a glass to release their aromatic properties. Muddlers may be purchased at good kitchenware retailers. They may be either wood or

plastic (purists prefer wood),
and should be long enough
to reach to the bottom of
the tallest glass you own.
Place your ingredients at the bottom of the
glass and grind gently but firmly for about 30
seconds. The leaves will release their minty-
ness, juice cells will joyfully burst, volatile oils
will be liberated, and the gates of paradise will
open.

To make a perfect mojito, you must use
guarapo, or sugar cane juice, available at
Hispanic grocery stores. There is simply no
substitute. Although the flavored variations
of the mojito will stand up to ordinary sugar,
don't even think about substitution in the
basic recipe. The absence of guarapo will be
noted. Traditionally, the mojito is served in a
tall, skinny glass—taller and skinnier even
than a Collins glass, although a Collins will
do in a pinch.

BASIC MOJITO

Technique is important here, perhaps more so than with other cocktails that can be combined in a blender or shaker.

2 oz. light rum
5–6 fresh mint leaves
3 drops bitters
1 lime, quartered
About 4 oz. guarapo
Club soda

Muddle mint leaves, bitters, and 3 lime quarters in the bottom of a chilled, tall glass. Leave everything right where it is. Fill glass to the top with crushed ice. Add rum and fill almost to the top with guarapo. Leave about 1/2 inch at the top of the glass. Top with club soda. Cover with a mixing glass and shake for a few seconds before serving with the remaining lime quarter, a sprig of fresh mint, or, if you can find one, a stick of sugar cane.

COSMOJITO

New York style meets Cuban flair in this hip marriage of two favorite classic cocktails.

1-1/2 oz. light rum
1-1/2 oz. Alizé Red Passion
1 lime, quartered
5–6 fresh mint leaves
1-1/2 oz. simple syrup OR 1 Tbs. superfine
  sugar
1-1/2 oz. cranberry juice
Club soda

Muddle 3 wedges of lime, mint leaves, and simple syrup (or sugar, if used) in the bottom of a tall glass. Fill glass with crushed ice. Add rum, Alizé Red Passion, cranberry juice, and club soda. Shake briefly and serve. Garnish with a slice of the remaining lime quarter.

Muddle ingredients in a mixing glass as described above. Add remaining ingredients except club soda, which you won't be using. Shake with cracked ice and strain into a chilled cocktail glass. Accessorize with a skinny little slice of designer lime.

FENI MOJITO

Feni is a liqueur distilled from the fruit (yes, fruit) of the cashew tree and produced in India. Its pleasantly tart, astringent taste makes it a perfect partner in the mojito.

1-1/4 oz. Kazkar Feni liqueur
2 apple slices (Granny Smith or other tart cooking apple)
2 tsp. superfine sugar
4–6 oz. apple juice
Club soda

Muddle apple slices and sugar together in a tall glass. Fill glass with ice and add Feni liqueur. Top with apple juice and finish with club soda. Shake to combine, and serve with a thin apple wedge and a thinner lime wedge. You will feel your karma changing as you sip this exotic cocktail.

LAVENDER MOJITO

2-1/2 oz. vanilla-flavored rum
3 lime wedges
2–3 sprigs of fresh lavender
5 fresh mint leaves
1 oz. simple syrup
Club soda

Muddle lime wedges, lavender sprigs, mint leaves, and simple syrup in the bottom of a tall glass. Fill glass with crushed ice. Add rum and club soda. Shake briefly and serve. Garnish with a crystallized violet or silk flower. Note: If you can't get your hands on fresh lavender, substitute a few drops of lavender-flavored Monin syrup.

LYCHEE MOJITO

1-1/2 oz. light rum
3 lime wedges
5–6 fresh mint leaves
1/2 oz. falernum
1/2 oz. lychee syrup (available at
www.lycheesonline.com)
Club soda

Muddle lime wedges, mint leaves, falernum, and lychee syrup in the bottom of a tall glass. Fill glass with crushed ice. Add rum and club soda. Shake briefly and serve. Garnish with a maraschino cherry skewered through a pitted, fresh lychee.

MANDARIN MOJITO

2 oz. mandarin orange-flavored vodka
1/4 lime, cut in wedges
5–6 fresh mint leaves
1/2 orange, cut into 3 wedges
1 oz. simple syrup
Club soda

Muddle lime, mint leaves, orange, and simple syrup in the bottom of a tall glass. Fill glass with crushed ice. Add vodka and club soda. Shake briefly and serve. Garnish with an orange wheel and a sprig of fresh mint. If the glass is full of fruit, remove one or two of the orange sections.

Mango Mojito

2-1/4 oz. mango-infused rum (see below)
5–6 fresh mint leaves
1 oz. fresh lime juice
1 oz. simple syrup
Club soda

Muddle mint leaves, lime juice, and simple syrup in the bottom of a tall glass. Fill glass with crushed ice. Add rum and club soda. Shake briefly and serve. Top with a slice of fresh mango.

To make mango-infused rum, you will need:

1-1/2 cups light rum
3/4 cup orange or lemon-flavored rum
3/4 cup vanilla-flavored rum
2 mangoes, peeled and chopped
1-inch piece of fresh ginger, peeled

Combine all ingredients in a glass container and leave in the refrigerator for a week. Strain into another container. Eat mangoes!

international party hot spot

THE ROSE BAR, SOUTH BEACH, MIAMI

In a city renowned for cool sophistication, the Delano Hotel stands out, from its all-white guest rooms to its landscaped "water salon." Tucked inside this dazzling edifice is the elegant Rose Bar, where one relaxes after a hard day of tanning or retail therapy with an ultra-hip signature cocktail. Razz Mojito, anyone?

Razz Mojito

2 oz. Bacardi Razz (raspberry-flavored) rum
1 tsp. brown sugar
3 lime wedges
5–6 fresh mint leaves
5 fresh raspberries
Club soda

Muddle brown sugar, lime wedges, and mint leaves in the bottom of a tall glass. Add raspberries and muddle briefly. They should be bruised enough to yield flavor without being completely mashed. Fill glass with crushed ice. Add rum and club soda. Shake briefly and serve. Garnish with a sprig of fresh mint. *Reproduced by kind permission of the Rose Bar (www.delano-hotel.com).*

CAIPIRINHAS AND CAIPIROSKAS

Ready for a little trip to *carnaval*? Brazil's national drink, the caipirinha (pronounced kai-pee-reen-ya), sambaed its way into history as a drink favored by field workers. Now it's become the hottest cocktail for the cool Copacabana set.

The principal ingredient of the caipirinha is cachaça, a spirit distilled from the juice of sugar cane. (Cachaça is nothing like its distant cousin rum, which is distilled from molasses.) When used in caipirinhas, the "newer" the spirit, the better—aged

cachaça can detract from the freshness of the pure sugar cane flavor.

Caipirinhas are also happily married to that most versatile of partners, the lime. And

Brazilian experts will tell you only white cane sugar should be used in preparation—never simple syrup or brown sugar. Use superfine white sugar. It usually dissolves quickly and doesn't require extensive mixing.

If you run out of cachaça, just switch to vodka, and you'll be drinking a caipiroska. Or if the only thing you have in the house is rum, you can make a caipirissima. So pretend you're at *carnaval*—improvise, be creative, and have fun!

BASIC CAIPIRINHA

2 oz. cachaça
1 lime, sliced and seeded
1 Tbs. superfine sugar

Muddle the lime and sugar in the bottom of a chilled old-fashioned glass until sugar dissolves. Fill glass with cracked ice. Pour cachaça over ice and stir to combine. Serve with a big gaudy lime wheel.

Note: Traditionally this cocktail is served very sweet (some recipes call for up to three table-spoons of sugar), so you will be forgiven for using a heavy hand with the sugar.

CAIPIRINHA DE TANGERINA

2 oz. cachaça
1/2 tangerine, peeled and sliced
1 Tbs. superfine sugar

Muddle the tangerine and sugar in the bottom of a chilled old-fashioned glass until sugar dissolves. Fill glass with cracked ice. Pour cachaça over ice and stir to combine. Serve with a tangerine slice.

FUZZY CAIPIROSKA

You might find yourself a little fuzzy around the edges after one or two of these!

1-1/2 oz. vodka
1/3 oz. peach schnapps
1 lime, sliced and seeded
Dash fresh peach puree
2 Tbs. superfine sugar

Muddle the lime, peach puree, and sugar in the bottom of a chilled old-fashioned glass until sugar dissolves. Fill glass with crushed ice. Pour vodka and schnapps over ice and stir to combine. Garnish with a fresh peach slice and serve with a straw.

GRAPEFRUIT AND GINGER CAIPIRINHA

2 oz. cachaça
1/2 cup peeled fresh grapefruit, cut in chunks
1 Tbs. grated fresh ginger
2 Tbs. superfine sugar
Splash of Cointreau

Muddle grapefruit, ginger, and sugar in a chilled old-fashioned glass until sugar dissolves. Add crushed ice and cachaça and stir to combine. Splash Cointreau over top. Serve with crystallized ginger.

KUMQUAT CAIPIRINHA

If you are fortunate enough to find yourself with a surplus of these snappy little cousins to the orange, try this recipe. Because they can be tart, adjust the sugar to taste.

2 oz. cachaça
4 kumquats, halved and seeded (try to do this over a glass so no juice will be lost)
1/2 lime, sliced and seeded
1 Tbs. superfine sugar

Muddle kumquats, lime, and sugar in the bottom of a chilled old-fashioned glass until sugar dissolves. Fill glass with crushed ice. Add cachaça and stir to combine. Decorate with whole kumquats on skewers.

STRAWBERRY CAIPIRINHA

2 oz. cachaça
1/4 oz. Chambord
4–5 fresh, ripe strawberries, hulled and
  roughly chopped, or frozen strawberries
  (frozen strawberries will be sweeter, so
  adjust sugar to taste)
1–2 tsp. superfine sugar

Muddle strawberries and sugar in the bottom of a chilled old-fashioned glass until sugar dissolves. Fill glass with crushed ice. Add cachaça and stir to combine. Drizzle Chambord over the top and garnish with a strawberry.

WILD BERRY CAIPIROSKA

We can think of no better cocktail to accompany a viewing of *Doctor Zhivago*. Its berry flavors are as wild as the Russian steppes.

2 oz. wild berry-flavored vodka
1/2 oz. crème de cassis or nalivka (a hard-to-find Russian berry-flavored liqueur)
4 blackberries, fresh or frozen
4 raspberries, fresh or frozen
1/2 lime, cut in wedges
1 tsp. superfine sugar

Muddle berries, lime, and sugar in the bottom of a chilled old-fashioned glass until sugar dissolves. Fill glass with crushed ice. Add vodka and stir to combine. Drizzle crème de cassis or nalivka over the top. Garnishing would be counterrevolutionary!

Pasha: *Come on, Comrades! Forward, comrades! Earth-shakers!*

DOCTOR ZHIVAGO (1965)

international party hot spot

TERRANEO BAR,
RIO DE JANEIRO

Flashy Rio—with its bodacious *carnaval*, stunning scenery, and high-rise-lined beaches described by one travel guide as "Manhattan with bikinis"—sizzles day and night.

Seeking a calm oasis in the *carnaval* frenzy? Drop into the J.W. Marriott on Rio's ritzy Avenida Atlantica, steps from Copacabana beach, and sip the Terraneo Bar's innovative take on Brazil's national drink.

CLASSIC CAIPIRINHA

4-1/2 oz. cachaça
1/3 oz. Grand Marnier
2 Tbs. superfine sugar
1 lime, peeled, sliced, and seeded (set aside peel)
Zest from 1/4 of the lime peel
About 1/2 cup ice cubes

Blend all ingredients except Grand Marnier until slushy. Pour into a chilled cocktail glass. Drizzle Grand Marnier over the top. Decorate with a few ribbons of lime peel and a lime wedge. *Reproduced by kind permission of Terraneo Bar, Rio de Janeiro (http://marriott.com/property/propertypage/RIOMC).*

for party czars (and czarinas) only

33 DEGREES AND BELOW—
VODKA DRINKS SO COLD THEY'RE HOT!

*The relationship between a Russian and
a bottle of vodka is almost mystical.*

RICHARD OWEN

Some things shouldn't be frozen. Champagne is one. And distilled spirits can't be frozen because of their high alcohol content. But vodka can be. In fact, after storage in the freezer, vodka exhibits an oily quality when poured that many drinkers favor.

So if you've burned out your ice maker, your blender, and yourself on frozen libations, don't despair. Simply mix up some of these chilly classics—they're sure to heat up the party!

You'll find the recipes in this section feature vodka, and most display a distinctly Russian flavor—ideal drinks for long Siberian nights. Stolichnaya and Moskovskaya are among the best known Russian vodkas. Poland, Sweden, Finland, and other countries also produce fine vodkas.

Tonight, we drink! *Za vashe zdorov'ye!* "To your health!"

VODKATINIS

MINT MARTINI

2 oz. vodka
1 oz. white crème de menthe

Shake with cracked ice and strain into a chilled cocktail glass. Garnish with a sprig of fresh mint. You may also rim the glass with peppermint-flavored sugar: a drop of peppermint extract to 1/4 cup sugar.

Nick Charles: *The important thing is the rhythm. Always have rhythm in your shaking. Now a Manhattan you always shake to fox-trot time, a Bronx to two-step time, a dry martini you always shake to waltz time.*

THE THIN MAN (1934)

RED VODKATINI

Think of this cocktail as a frozen-tini hybrid.

2 oz. vodka
1 oz. dry vermouth
Dash of crème de cassis

Shake vodka and vermouth with cracked ice and strain into an old-fashioned glass filled with crushed ice. Splash crème de cassis over the top and garnish with a very un-Russian orange slice.

SAFE HOUSE MARTINI

Take a break from your top-secret mission and kick back in the nearest safe house with a chilled martini and a sizzling double agent. Strive for better international relations.

2-1/2 oz. vodka—straight from the freezer
1/2 oz. sweet vermouth, chilled
Dash cherry juice

Shake vodka with cracked ice and strain into a chilled cocktail glass. Add vermouth, but do not mix. Drizzle cherry juice over the top and drop in two fresh pitted cherries.

James Bond: *My dear girl, there are some things that just aren't done, such as drinking Dom Pérignon '53 above the temperature of 38 degrees Fahrenheit. That's just as bad as listening to the Beatles without earmuffs!*

GOLDFINGER (1964)

SOUTH BEACH MARTINI

We don't know if this is allowed on the famous diet of the same name, but it manages to squeeze the taste of Florida into a cocktail glass.

1-1/4 oz. orange-flavored vodka
1-1/4 oz. lemon-flavored vodka
1/2 oz. Cointreau
Lemon sugar (see pages 14-15)

Moisten the rim of a chilled cocktail glass with a cut orange. Spin glass in lemon sugar to coat rim. Shake remaining ingredients with cracked ice and strain into prepared glass. Decorate with little ribbons of orange and lemon peel.

WATERMELON MARTINI

1 oz. citrus vodka (orange or lemon)
1 oz. melon liqueur
1/2 cup fresh watermelon chunks
1/2 oz. fresh lemon juice

Muddle watermelon chunks and lemon juice in a cocktail shaker or mixing glass. Add vodka, melon liqueur, and cracked ice. Shake well. Strain into a chilled cocktail glass. Serve with a very thin wedge of watermelon—with rind on.

international party hot spot

In Las Vegas, the eternal party city, Caesar's Palace is the perfect forum. Once inside, follow the beat—and the crowd—to PURE Nightclub, where the Puretini is *the* drink. It's pure cool!

PURETINI

3 oz. Stoli Razberi vodka
1 oz. sweet-and-sour mix
1 oz. Sprite or lemon-lime soda
Splash blue curaçao liqueur

Shake all ingredients with cracked ice and strain into a chilled cocktail glass. Garnish with a twist of lemon peel—just enough to look cool and accessorize this otherwise splendidly minimalist creation. *Reproduced by kind permission of PURE Nightclub (www.harrahs.com/casinos/caesars-palace/casino-misc/pure-nightclub-detail.html).*

MORE ICY COOLERS

ARCTIC CIRCLE

1 oz. vodka
1/2 oz. lime juice
Ginger ale

Shake vodka and lime juice with cracked ice and strain into an iced highball glass. Fill with ginger ale and stir to combine. Decorate with a sprig of fresh mint and an icicle swizzle stick.

FRENCH FLAMINGO

1 oz. black currant-flavored
vodka
1 oz. Cointreau
3/4 oz. fresh lime juice
3/4 oz. fresh pomegranate juice

Shake with cracked ice and strain into a chilled cocktail glass. Serve with a twist of lime peel and a flamingo-shaped swizzle stick.

FROZEN MELON BALL

1-1/2 oz. melon liqueur
1/2 oz. vodka
2 oz. pineapple juice
1 tsp. fresh lime juice

Shake all ingredients with cracked ice and strain into a chilled cocktail glass filled with crushed ice. Garnish with a skewer of frozen melon balls and a short straw.

LEMON DROP

1-1/2 oz. lemon-flavored vodka
3/4 oz. fresh lemon juice
1 tsp. simple syrup
Lemon sugar (see pages 14-15)

Moisten rim of a chilled cocktail glass with a cut lemon. Spin glass in lemon sugar to coat rim. Shake remaining ingredients with cracked ice and strain into prepared glass.

For a more austere version, omit simple

syrup, lemon juice, and sugar and serve with a sugared lemon wedge. Pucker up, baby!

PETIT ZINC

Sorry, but it's a myth: there are no bars made of zinc in France, or anywhere else, and never have been. The characteristic French metal bars are actually made of an alloy of lead and tin. But we couldn't call a cocktail the "Petit Lead."

1 oz. vodka
3/4 oz. Cointreau
1/2 oz. sweet vermouth
*1/2 oz. fresh orange juice, preferably from
   Seville oranges*

Stir all ingredients with cracked ice and strain into a chilled cocktail glass. Garnish with a cherry or orange slice.

SOVIET COCKTAIL

The Soviet Union may be history, but we say *"da!"* to this legacy.

1-1/2 oz. Russian vodka
1/2 oz. dry vermouth
1/2 oz. dry sherry

Shake all ingredients with cracked ice and strain into a chilled cocktail glass. Garnish with a twist of lemon peel, twisted over the glass to release the volatile oils.

international party hot spot

DADY'O, CANCUN

In Mexico's playground, the most happening nightlife in town is Dady'O, with its rock-and-roll Dady Rock club and super-swank O Ultra Lounge for VIPs. Their signature cocktails, such as the Wild Daddy, are famous with spring breakers the world over.

WILD DADDY COCKTAIL

1-1/2 oz. vodka
1-1/2 oz. butterscotch liqueur
1-1/2 oz. milk

Shake all ingredients with cracked ice and strain into a chilled cocktail glass. *Reproduced by kind permission of Dady'O (www.dadyo.com.mx).*

international party hot spot

It's a little bit of the Kremlin in downtown Las Vegas. A tribute to all things vodka, Red Square restaurant, voted "Best Bar in America" in 2000 by *Playboy* magazine, is located inside Mandalay Bay Hotel, right on the Strip. Sip your Stoli at the ice bar (yes, the bar surface is made of ice!), or sample over 100 types of vodka in a private locker (hopefully not all at once). Nibble a Siberian nacho, or indulge in Beluga caviar. You might think you're stepping back in time to the Russian revolution—until a familiar celebrity drops in for a drink!

CHERNOBYL

Red Square bartenders garnish this cocktail with a three-eyed candy fish! If you can't find mutant candy, feel free to deform your favorite gummy creature any way you like.

3/4 oz. Absolut vodka
3/4 oz. Moskovskaya vodka
3/4 oz. Stolichnaya vodka
3/4 oz. triple sec
1 oz. cranberry juice

Pour ingredients into an ice-filled pint glass and garnish with gummy candy. *Reproduced by kind permission of Red Square, Las Vegas (www.man dalaybay.com/dining/restaurants_ red_square.aspx).*

international party hot spot

Stuck at the bottom of the world and looking for a place to party? Planet Champagne Bar easily qualifies as one of the hottest spots south of the equator. Tucked inside Cape Town's splendidly Victorian landmark, the Mount Nelson Hotel, Planet is anything but stuffy. As the name suggests, Planet specializes in champagne (on its own or mixed in cocktails) and exotic and ultra-hip drinks. While you're celebrity-spotting, experience one of Planet's justifiably world-famous frozen delights—or try one of their signature drinks, like Liquid Cocaine. It's a sure-fire party starter!

LIQUID COCAINE

1 oz. vodka
2 oz. Red Bull
Champagne or sparkling wine

Mix vodka and Red Bull gently in a chilled champagne glass. Fill with your favorite champagne or sparkling wine. Garnish with a sexy red maraschino cherry. *Reproduced by kind permission of Planet Champagne Bar (www.mountnelson.co.za/web/ocap/ocap_c4b4_planet.jsp).*

got the blues?
we can help!

A RHAPSODY OF DRINKS IN SHADES
OF CARIBBEAN BLUE

*My aunts lived on liquor and seldom felt like
eating much. . . .There was one emotional outlet
my people always had when they had the blues.*

ETHEL WATERS

Reminiscent of sea and sky, these azure creations are sure to chase the clouds away. Our secret ingredient (in most of these recipes): blue curaçao (pronounced "cure-a-sow") liqueur. Produced on the Netherland Antilles island of Curaçao, 35 miles north of Venezuela, this clear liquid also comes in green, orange, and red; its flavor is that of bitter oranges.

BLUE COSMOPOLITAN

If a Cosmo girl ever had the blues, this would be the sure-fire antidote.

2 oz. lemon-flavored vodka
1 oz. blue curaçao liqueur
1/2 oz. grapefruit juice
1/2 oz. simple syrup
Blue sugar (see page 14)

Frost the rim of a chilled cocktail glass with blue sugar. Stir together remaining ingredients in a mixing glass and strain into prepared glass. Garnish with a razor-thin twist of orange peel.

Frost rim of a large, chilled goblet with blue sugar. Blend remaining ingredients with about 1 cup of ice cubes in blender until slushy. Pour into prepared glass. This version calls for a more robust wheel of orange, perhaps skewered with a maraschino cherry.

BLUE HAWAIIAN

You would be forgiven if you accused us of slipping in a recipe that sounds suspiciously like a blue version of the Piña Colada. Regardless, you'll be crooning like the King himself after one or two of these.

1 oz. light rum
1 oz. blue curaçao liqueur
2 oz. pineapple juice
1 oz. cream of coconut
About 1 cup ice cubes

Blend all ingredients in blender until slushy. Pour into a chilled parfait glass. You can go "classic" and garnish with the traditional pineapple chunks and maraschino cherry, or get creative and decorate with a bright artificial flower stuck on a swizzle stick.

For a Blue Hawaiian Screw, substitute vodka for rum and eliminate cream of coconut. Add more pineapple juice to taste.

BLUE LAGOON

This no-fooling drink was reportedly created by Andy MacElhone, son of the late, great Harry MacElhone of Harry's New York Bar in Paris.

1-1/2 oz. blue vodka (if unavailable, use
plain vodka)
1-1/2 oz. gin (preferably Plymouth)
1-1/2 oz. blue curaçao liqueur
1-1/2 oz. fresh lime juice
1-1/2 oz. simple syrup

 Mix ingredients with cracked ice in a cocktail shaker. Strain into a Collins glass filled with crushed ice. Garnish with a ribbon of lime peel. You can also try this drink with lemon or orange-flavored vodkas. If this seems like a lot of alcohol for you, add more ice and divide in two.

BLUE LIGHT SPECIAL

Attention Kmart shoppers! Apple, pineapple, and orange—it's an entire fruit salad for the price of one drink. Not to be missed!

1 oz. apple schnapps
1 oz. blue curaçao liqueur
4 oz. pineapple juice
About 1 cup ice cubes

Blend all ingredients in blender until slushy. Pour into a chilled jelly glass or heavy tumbler. Don't bother with garnish—this is a "no frills" drink.

BLUE MARGARITA

1-1/2 oz. silver tequila
1/2 oz. blue curaçao liqueur
Juice of 1/2 lime
Blue-tinted salt

Moisten the rim of chilled margarita glass with a piece of cut lime and spin glass rim in salt. Mix all ingredients in a cocktail shaker with cracked ice. Strain into salted glass and garnish with a lime wedge.

TO MAKE FROZEN:

Combine all ingredients (except salt) with about 1 cup ice cubes and blend until slushy. Pour into prepared glass.

BLUE MOJITO

2 oz. light rum
1 oz. Hpnotiq liqueur
6 fresh mint leaves
Club soda

Shake all ingredients except club soda, strain into an iced old-fashioned glass, and top with club soda. Garnish with a sprig of fresh mint.

BLUE WHALE

Fun fact: Adult blue whales weigh between 200,000 and 300,000 pounds, and consume up to four tons of krill per day. Don't bring a blue whale to the "all-you-can-eat" seafood buffet—he will embarrass you. It is perfectly OK to order this cocktail at any restaurant, however.

1-1/2 oz. vodka
1-1/2 oz. blue curaçao liqueur
1-1/2 oz. orange juice
1-1/2 oz. pineapple juice

1/2 oz. simple syrup
Juice of 1/2 lemon

(You may substitute 1-1/2 oz. sweet-and-sour mix for the simple syrup and lemon juice, but we don't recommend it.)

TRADITIONAL METHOD:

Shake all ingredients vigorously in a cocktail shaker filled with cracked ice. Strain into a chilled Collins glass and garnish with an orange wheel.

FROZEN METHOD:

Blend ingredients with about 1 cup ice cubes in blender until slushy. Pour into a large, chilled goblet.

CARIBBEAN BLUES

A tropical-yet-glacial variation on the martini theme.

3/4 oz. vodka
1/2 oz. blue curaçao liqueur
1/2 oz. dry vermouth

Mix all ingredients in a mixing glass with cracked ice. Strain into an old-fashioned glass filled with crushed ice.

Sylvia Blair: *Does he look like an interior decorator to you?*
Peg Costello: *No. He looks like one of those men who suddenly switched to vodka!*

DESK SET, 1957

CLÉMENT CREOLE COSMOPOLITAN

This Martinique import is light and cool, like a refreshing breeze.

2-1/2 oz. light rum
1 oz. Clément Creole Shrubb or curaçao
1/2 oz. cranberry juice
1/2 oz. fresh lime juice

Shake all ingredients with cracked ice and strain into a chilled cocktail glass. Decorate with dainty curls of lime peel.

DREAMIN' CARIBBEAN

Properly prepared, this cocktail will look exactly like the varied, jewel-like, blue/green hues of the Caribbean Sea. It is worth the trouble.

3/4 oz. light rum
1-1/2 oz. melon liqueur
3/4 oz. pineapple juice
1-1/2 oz. blue curaçao liqueur
3/4 oz. cream of coconut

Combine rum, melon liqueur, and pineapple juice in a cocktail shaker filled with cracked ice. Shake vigorously. Strain and pour into a chilled, saucer-shaped glass. Rinse shaker and refill with cracked ice. Add blue curaçao liqueur and cream of coconut; once again, shake vigorously. Pour a small amount of curaçao/cream of coconut mixture down the inner rim of the glass, and agitate gently—ingredients should swirl but not blend. Repeat until all of the mixture is used.

ISLAND PASSION

Properly prepared, this cocktail will appear dark purple or black.

1/2 oz. vodka
1/2 oz. blue curaçao
1/2 oz. Passoá liqueur
1-1/2 oz. cranberry juice
1-1/2 oz. fresh orange juice

Shake with cracked ice and strain into a chilled cocktail glass. Serve without accompaniment—to inflame tropical passions.

PURPLE MARTINI

So smooth, you wouldn't know it's made with gin.

2 oz. Beefeater Gin
1/2 oz. blue curaçao
1/2 oz. strawberry liqueur

Stir all ingredients with cracked ice and strain into a chilled cocktail glass. Garnish with a twist of orange peel. *Reproduced by kind permission of The Court of Two Sisters (see pages 33-34).*

SCUBA-TINI
Don't drink and dive!

2-1/2 oz. vodka
1/2 oz. blue curaçao
1/4 oz. fresh lemon juice
Rubber shark

Shake all ingredients (except rubber shark) with cracked ice and strain into a chilled cocktail glass. Serve with the rubber shark in the glass.

WILD BLUE YONDER

1-1/2 oz. vodka
1/4 oz. peach schnapps
1/4 oz. blue curaçao liqueur

TRADITIONAL METHOD:

Mix ingredients with cracked ice in a cocktail shaker. Strain into a chilled cocktail glass or serve on the rocks. Garnish with a fresh peach slice.

FROZEN METHOD:

Blend ingredients with about 1 cup ice cubes in blender until slushy. Pour into a large, chilled goblet.

too cool for school

GROWN-UP PARTY COCKTAILS, FROM
COUNTRY-CLUB SUAVE TO NIGHTCLUB SEXY

Alma: *Then I'm going to go back to my
home town in Oregon, and I'm going to build
a house for my mother and myself, and join
the country club and take up golf.*

FROM HERE TO ETERNITY (1953)

You may remember your parents guzzling these classics, or you may have tried them yourself. One thing's certain: they've all come back in a big way. What used to be the rage at the country club is now the hottest thing at the nightclub.

So dust off the vintage glasses—you know, the frosted ones with the etching and the gold trim—and mix up a batch of these tried-and-true favorites.

OLD SCHOOL CLASSICS

BAY BREEZE

2 oz. vodka
Pineapple juice
Cranberry juice

Pour vodka into an iced highball glass. Fill partway with pineapple juice and top with cranberry juice.

BERMUDA RUM SWIZZLE

Just the thing after a hard day on the golf course. Best enjoyed at the 19th hole.

2 oz. dark rum
1 oz. fresh lime juice
1 oz. orange juice
1 oz. pineapple juice
1/4 oz. falernum (grenadine may be substituted, but it won't taste the same)

Shake all ingredients and strain into an iced highball glass. Garnish with an orange slice and a cherry.

CAPE CODDER

1-1/2 oz. vodka
Cranberry juice

Pour vodka into an iced highball glass. Fill with cranberry juice and serve with a lime wedge. For a lighter drink, use half cranberry juice and half club soda.

CUBA LIBRE

Sing along with the Andrews Sisters'
1945 hit, "Rum and Coca-Cola."

2 oz. light rum
Juice of 1/2 lime
Coca-Cola

Pour lime juice into an iced highball glass,
then add rum and Coca-Cola. Stir gently and
serve with a lime wedge.

For a Cuba Pintada, substitute club soda for
Coke and add just a splash of Coke at the end
of mixing—just enough to lightly color the
liquid.

The Cuba Campechana uses half club soda
and half Coca-Cola.

GIN AND WHAT?

Traditionally, a proper British Gin and It was served at room temperature, without ice. Served thusly, it probably wouldn't have many fans today. Here is an updated version.

1-1/2 oz. gin
1-1/2 oz. sweet vermouth

Stir with cracked ice and strain into a chilled cocktail glass. Add a dash of bitters if desired and garnish with a twist of orange peel. May also be served in an old-fashioned glass on the rocks.

LIME RICKEY

The Rickey family of refreshing, citrusy coolers deserves better recognition. They are rumored to have originated in the seaside town of Wildwood, New Jersey.

1-1/2 oz. gin
Juice of 1/2 lime, fruit reserved
Club soda

Squeeze lime into a chilled highball glass (beware of seeds) and drop fruit in glass. Add gin. Fill glass with cracked ice and top with club soda.

Try variations using vodka, sloe gin, or tequila.

MINT JULEP

In addition to an over-the-top hat and a smart pair of opera glasses, this is the only accessory you'll need at the Kentucky Derby.

4 oz. Kentucky bourbon
5–6 fresh mint leaves
1 tsp. simple syrup

Muddle mint leaves and simple syrup in the bottom of a chilled highball glass. Fill glass with crushed ice, then add bourbon. Stir until glass is frosted (this will be easier if using the traditional silver cup favored by Run-for-the-Roses purists). Garnish with 4 more mint sprigs and fresh fruit (your choice). Serve with 2 straws.

ORANGE BLOSSOM

2 oz. gin
1 oz. orange juice
1/4 tsp. superfine sugar

Stir with cracked ice and strain into a chilled cocktail glass. Garnish with an orange slice. The perfect luncheon accompaniment, especially with those little finger sandwiches with the crusts cut off.

PIMM'S CUP

Unquestionably the beverage of choice if you are an aficionado of five-day cricket matches. Pimm's No. 1 is a gin-based liqueur infused with fruits, herbs, and aromatics. So this cocktail has the added benefit of being good for you!

2 oz. Pimm's No. 1
Lemon-lime soda

Pour Pimm's into an iced highball glass and

fill with lemon-lime soda. Garnish with a long finger of cucumber.

For a **Royal Pimm's Cup**, substitute champagne for lemon-lime soda. Jolly refreshing!

PLANTER'S PUNCH

This seems a quaint antebellum holdover. That is, until you have a couple and they punch your lights out.

2 oz. light rum
1 oz. dark rum
2 tsp. simple syrup
Juice of 2 limes
Soda water
Few drops of bitters

Pour light rum, syrup, and lime juice into a highball glass filled with crushed ice and stir until glass frosts. Add dark rum. Fill with soda water and top with bitters. Garnish with fresh fruit and sugared mint sprigs.

SAZERAC COCKTAIL

This Big Easy classic was originally prescribed as a tonic by an 18th-century French Quarter druggist named Peychaud, who believed everyone could benefit from his "bitters."

1-1/4 oz. rye whiskey
Herbsaint—a non-toxic absinthe substitute
   produced in (you guessed it) New Orleans
1/4 oz. simple syrup or 1 tsp. sugar
4 dashes Peychaud's bitters
3 dashes Angostura Bitters

Chill an old-fashioned glass in the freezer. Pour a few drops of Herbsaint into the glass and swirl to coat glass. Pour out excess and set the glass on a bed of ice. Stir remaining ingredients with cracked ice until they are completely chilled. Strain into prepared glass. Garnish with a twist of lemon. *Reproduced by kind permission of The Court of Two Sisters (see pages 33-34).*

SCOTCH MIST

2 oz. Scotch whisky

Pour Scotch whisky over crushed ice in an old-fashioned glass. Add a generous twist of lemon peel. Serve with two short straws. If you listen closely, you will hear the pipes.

SEA BREEZE

1-1/2 oz. vodka
2 oz. cranberry juice
2 oz. grapefruit juice

Shake well with cracked ice and strain into an iced highball glass. Garnish with a lime slice.

SINGAPORE SLING

*Raffles stands for all the fables
of the exotic East.*

SOMERSET MAUGHAM

This famous drink was first created in that bastion of British colonial elegance, Raffles Hotel. Named for Singapore's founder, Sir Stamford Raffles, this Asian landmark first opened its doors in 1887, and quickly became popular with both British colonials and literati. Among its famous denizens: Herman Hesse, Noel Coward, Joseph Conrad, and the indefatigable Mr. Maugham, after whom a suite was eventually named. As for the legend that the last tiger in Singapore was shot and killed under a billiard table in the hotel's bar . . . the hotel's management neither confirms nor denies this story.

1-1/2 oz. gin
1/2 oz. cherry brandy or Heering Cherry
  liqueur
Few drops Bénédictine
Juice of 1/2 lemon
Soda water

Shake all ingredients except soda water with cracked ice and strain into an iced highball glass. Fill with soda water and garnish with a lemon slice. If more sweetness is desired, add a little simple syrup.

international party hot spot

The Miami audience is the greatest audience in the world.

JACKIE GLEASON (1966)

A Miami Beach landmark for more than 90 years, Joe's Stone Crab is the place to be seen. Past patrons have included J. Edgar Hoover, Al Capone, the Duke and Duchess of Windsor, and Will Rogers. Its signature dessert is the Key Lime Pie, so it's no surprise that Joe's featured cocktails also highlight the petite, piquant key lime! Try mixing up a batch of these refreshingly tangy delights for your next barbecue or outdoor "do."

KEY LIME MARTINI

1-1/2 oz. Grey Goose vodka
1-1/2 oz. triple sec
1 oz. key lime mix (opposite)
1 graham cracker, crushed

Moisten rim of a chilled cocktail glass with triple sec and spin glass in graham cracker crumbs. Shake remaining ingredients with cracked ice and strain into prepared glass. Garnish with a perfect lime slice.

KEY LIME FIZZ

1-1/2 oz. Bacardi Limón rum
1-1/2 oz. key lime mix (opposite)
Sprite or other lemon-lime soda

Shake rum and key lime mix with cracked ice and strain into an iced old-fashioned glass. Fill with lemon-lime soda and garnish with another one of those perfect lime wheels.

KEY LIME MIX

Use this handy mix to create your own key lime concoctions. Fresh lime juice is always preferable to bottled, but the bottled product is an acceptable substitute. You may think this recipe (which makes just under 1/2 gallon) is too much, but it disappears fast!

2-1/2 cups (20 oz.) simple syrup
1-1/4 cups (10 oz.) egg white
  (or pasteurized egg white substitute)
4 cups (32 oz.) lime juice

Shake simple syrup, egg white, and a small amount of lime juice in a 64-oz. container until blended. Add remaining lime juice and shake until well mixed. Refrigerate until needed. *Special thanks to the folks at Joe's Stone Crab for sharing these party-perfect recipes (www.joesstonecrab.com).*

THE COLLINS CLAN— MEET THE WHOLE GANG

This is one diverse and adaptable family. Beginning with the patriarch, Tom Collins, whose venerable ancestors include gin and tonic, whiskey sour, and gin fizz, you will find multi-generations of summer coolers. Like every good family, the Collinses have their own signature glassware: they're tall and usually hold 12 ounces. Highball glasses will do in a pinch, however. Once again, we are compelled to speak out against packaged mix, unless you have no other choice.

BASIC TOM COLLINS

2 oz. gin
1 tsp. superfine sugar
Juice of 1/2 lemon
Club soda

Place sugar and lemon juice in an iced high-ball glass. Add gin and fill with club soda. Stir and garnish with a lemon wedge and a cherry.

LET THEM GO FORTH AND MULTIPLY:

CRANBERRY COLLINS

1-1/2 oz. gin
1/2 oz. cranberry juice
Juice of a lime
Club soda

Pour gin, cranberry juice, and lime juice into an iced highball glass. Fill with club soda and stir gently. If this isn't sweet enough for you, substitute lemon-lime soda for all or part of the club soda.

JOHN COLLINS

Substitute bourbon for gin.

PEDRO COLLINS

Also called a Rum Collins, this one substitutes light rum for gin.

SANDY COLLINS

Substitute Scotch whisky for gin. Also known as a Scotch Collins.

SLOE GIN FIZZ
(Yes, it's a Collins!)

2 oz. sloe gin
1/2 oz. fresh lemon juice
1 tsp. simple syrup
Club soda

Shake all ingredients except club soda with cracked ice and strain into an iced highball glass. Fill to the top with club soda. Garnish with a lemon slice.

Invent your own "Collins creation" using the basic ratios described above. See how many you can come up with.

international party hot spot

FALCON, LOS ANGELES

Named for Falcon's Lair, Hollywood home of silent movie legend Rudolph Valentino, this contemporary haven of style, conveniently located near the landmark Saharan Motel, simply oozes glamour. Aspiring Rat Packers are encouraged to sample the Dirty Sue—that's a filthy martini!

DIRTY SUE

3 oz. gin or vodka

*3/4 oz. Dirty Sue bottled olive juice
(using bottled juice ensures you won't
be using all the juice from your olive
jar, leaving your olives high and dry).*

Shake or stir—your choice—with
cracked ice and strain into a chilled
cocktail glass. Garnish with two
olives. *Reproduced by kind permission
of Falcon, Los Angeles (www.falcons
lair.com).*

decadent dessert delights

GRAND FINALES

Dessert is probably the most important stage of the meal, since it will be the last thing your guests remember before they pass out all over the table.

WILLIAM POWELL

Dessert drinks have come a long way from the days of speakeasy mixologists splashing liqueur and cream into home-brewed spirits to make them more appealing. Today's confections are well-bred, wickedly wonderful, and worth every calorie. From the dessert martini (the perfect nightcap) to all-out, postprandial extravaganzas, this is the way to have your cake and eat it, too. On second thought, who needs cake?

BANANA RUM CREAM

1-1/2 oz. dark rum
1-1/2 oz. crème de bananes
1 oz. cream

Shake well with cracked ice and strain into a chilled cocktail glass. If desired, rim glass with *turbinado* (raw sugar) or light brown sugar.

BLACK-AND-WHITE MARTINI

2-1/2 oz. vanilla-flavored vodka
3/4 oz. crème de cacao

Shake well with cracked ice and strain into a chilled cocktail glass. Drop half a split vanilla bean into the glass and serve with nonpareil candy.

BLACK RUSSIAN

1-1/2 oz. vodka
3/4 oz. Kahlúa Liqueur

Shake well with cracked ice and strain into an iced old-fashioned glass.

Add a few drops of fresh lemon juice, and—presto!—a Black Magic.

For a White Russian, combine 2 oz. vodka with 1 oz. Kahlúa Liqueur and 1 oz. cream. Shake with cracked ice and strain into an iced old-fashioned glass.

BRANDY ALEXANDER

This cocktail is one of the oldest known dessert drinks. A variation is prepared with gin instead of brandy.

1 oz. brandy
1 oz. crème de cacao
1 oz. heavy cream
Nutmeg

Shake well with cracked ice and strain into an iced cocktail glass. Garnish with grated nutmeg.

BROKEN HEART MARTINI

While we can't promise that this cocktail will cure a broken heart, it might take the sting out of having one for a little while.

2-1/2 oz. black currant-flavored vodka
1/2 oz. Godiva chocolate liqueur
1/4 tsp. cocoa powder
1 Tbs. sugar

Mix cocoa powder and sugar in a saucer. Moisten the rim of a chilled cocktail glass with an orange slice. Dip glass in sugar-cocoa mixture to coat rim. Shake remaining ingredients with cracked ice and strain into prepared glass. Decorate with an orange slice and a small cluster of black currants.

international party hot spot

LA BUENA VIDA, AKUMAL

What's better than the hottest party town in the Western hemisphere? One that hasn't been discovered yet! When you've had enough of the non-stop action in Cancun, or if you just want to try something a little off the beaten path, drive down the coast of the Mexican Riviera to Akumal. This charming paradise is filled with cafés and bars that haven't been trampled by throngs of tourists. Don't miss La Buena Vida; this inviting restaurant serves up authentic Yucatanean specialty dishes and one-of-a-kind cocktails guaranteed to cool.

BUENA VIDA COCKTAIL

1/2 oz. coffee liqueur
1/2 oz. crème de cacao
1/2 oz. Grand Marnier
About 1 cup ice cubes

Blend all ingredients until slushy. Pour into a chilled goblet and garnish with a pineapple wedge and a cherry. Now you're living the good life! *Reproduced by kind permission of La Buena Vida (www.akumalinfo.com/la_buena_vida.html).*

CARA-MELLOW MARTINI

Whip up a spun-sugar fantasy—the martini never had it so sweet.

INGREDIENTS FOR FOUR GLASSES:

10 oz. vanilla-flavored vodka, chilled
2 oz. white crème de cacao
1/2 cup granulated sugar
1 cup water
1 vanilla bean, split lengthwise

Heat the sugar and water on low heat in a heavy saucepan. Stir until sugar dissolves. Bring to a boil and remove from the heat when the mixture thickens and turns golden. Set aside (no stirring!).

Scrape inside of vanilla bean into cocktail shaker and add chilled vodka, crème de cacao, and cracked ice. Shake well and strain into chilled martini glasses. Using a fork, pull strands of caramel out of the saucepan and twirl them around each glass. Don't worry if filaments of caramel land in the drink.

CHERRY VANILLA CLOUD

2-1/2 oz. vanilla-flavored vodka
1/2 oz. cherry brandy or Heering Cherry
* liqueur*
1 oz. cream

Shake well with cracked ice and strain into a chilled cocktail glass. Garnish with a maraschino cherry. If desired, rim cocktail glass with pink vanilla-flavored sugar.

For a **Cherry Vanilla Martini**, omit cream.

DEATH BY CHOCOLATE

If you gotta go, it might as well be with one of these in your hand!

3/4 oz. vanilla-flavored vodka
3/4 oz. crème de cacao
3/4 oz. Irish cream liqueur
1 scoop chocolate ice cream (don't skimp on
* the quality here)*
About 1 cup ice cubes

Blend all ingredients until smooth and pour into a chilled parfait glass. Garnish with shaved chocolate and a dollop of whipped cream sprinkled with cocoa powder.

ESPRESSO MARTINI

1-1/2 oz. vodka
1/2 oz. crème de cacao
1/2 oz. Kahlúa Liqueur
1 oz. cold espresso

Shake with cracked ice and strain into a chilled cocktail glass. Garnish with espresso beans and a twist of lemon peel.

GATSBY

*First you take a drink, then the drink takes
a drink, then the drink takes you.*

F. SCOTT FITZGERALD

3/4 oz. amaretto
3/4 oz. white crème de cacao
2 oz. cream

Shake with cracked ice and strain into a
chilled cocktail glass. Garnish with a few slivered, blanched almonds or shavings of white
chocolate.

GOLDEN CADILLAC

Galliano is a sweet combination of
vanilla, anise, and herbs.

1-1/2 oz. white crème de cacao
3/4 oz. Galliano
1-1/2 oz. cream

Shake well with cracked ice and strain into a
chilled cocktail glass.

MUDSLIDE

3/4 oz. vodka
3/4 oz. Irish cream liqueur
3/4 oz. Kahlúa Liqueur

Shake all ingredients with cracked ice and strain into a chilled cocktail glass. Garnish with chocolate curls or cocoa powder.

TO SERVE FROZEN:

Blend all ingredients with about 1 cup ice cubes until smooth. Pour into a chilled parfait glass.

PEACH MELBA FREEZE

Peach Melba is arguably the most famous of stone fruit dessert recipes. French chef Auguste Escoffier created the dish in the 1890s to commemorate the visit of opera diva Dame Nellie Melba to London's Savoy Hotel. Here is our interpretation of this sweet favorite.

3/4 oz. peach schnapps
3/4 oz. Chambord
3/4 oz. Frangelico
1 scoop vanilla ice cream
1/2 fresh peach, peeled and sliced
About 1 cup ice cubes

Blend all ingredients until smooth. Pour into a chilled parfait glass. Garnish with peach slices and a dollop of whipped cream.

PINK LADY

We recommend using pasteurized egg white to prepare this cocktail.

1-1/2 oz. gin
1 tsp. grenadine
1 tsp. cream
1 egg white (or 3 Tbs. pasteurized egg white
  substitute)

Shake it up with cracked ice. Then shake it some more. Think you've shaken enough? Keep on shaking. When you can truly shake no more, strain into a chilled cocktail glass. It should come out frothy, like a wisp of lingerie.

PINK SQUIRREL

The delicate almond flavor in this cocktail comes from the addition of crème de noyaux—made from the pits of peaches and apricots. Don't be tempted to substitute amaretto; its flavor will overpower the drink.

3/4 oz. white crème de cacao
3/4 oz. crème de noyaux
3/4 oz. cream

Shake with cracked ice and strain into a chilled cocktail glass. Garnish with a few slivered, blanched almonds.

SOMBRERO

Like all great cocktails, the Sombrero is simple and sublime—and subject to endless variations.

2 oz. Tia Maria or Kahlúa Liqueur
1 oz. cream

This can be served layered, with the liqueur at the bottom of the glass and the cream floated on top, or combined. Serve in an iced old-fashioned glass.

If you use amaretto, you'll have an **Almond Sombrero**.

Try with Frangelico for a Hazelnut Sombrero.

For a Cinnamon Sombrero, substitute cinnamon schnapps.

How about Grand Marnier? That will give you a Creamsicle (an Orange Sombrero).

Now you try.

TOASTED ALMOND

1-1/2 oz. Kahlúa Liqueur
1-1/2 oz. amaretto
1-1/2 oz. cream

Beginning with Kahlúa and ending with cream on top, layer ingredients in a chilled pony or pousse café glass by pouring the liquid over the back of a spoon. Use a different spoon for each ingredient, and don't allow the spoon to touch the liquid already in the glass.

TOBLERONE

No need to scale the Alps for a taste of this sweet Swiss treat.

1 oz. Frangelico
1 oz. Irish cream liqueur
1 oz. Kahlúa Liqueur
1 Tbs. sugar
1 Tbs. crushed hazelnuts
Chocolate syrup
2 oz. cream
1 Tbs. honey
About 1 cup ice

Mix sugar and hazelnuts in a saucer. Moisten rim of a chilled parfait glass with Frangelico and dip glass in hazelnut-sugar mixture to coat rim. Carefully drizzle a few ribbons of chocolate syrup down the inside of the glass. Blend remaining ingredients until smooth and pour into prepared glass, taking care not to disturb chocolate syrup. Garnish with crushed hazelnuts and cocoa powder.

international party hot spot

When you're in search of the coolest vibe down under, look no further than the Water Bar in Sydney's BLUE hotel. Situated in the curiously-named wharf district of Woolloomooloo (an aboriginal word possibly meaning "place of plenty"), BLUE is where the elite meet to treat themselves to the latest, greatest cocktails on the edge of the Pacific.

THE VANILLA PASSION

1-1/2 oz. Cariel vodka (a premium
  vanilla vodka from Sweden)
1 oz. passion fruit puree
1/2 oz. apple juice
1 tsp. fresh lime juice
1 tsp. fresh or canned passion fruit pulp
Vanilla sugar (see page 14)

Moisten the rim of a chilled cocktail glass with a little passion fruit puree. Spin glass in vanilla sugar to coat rim. Drop the passion fruit pulp into the bottom of the glass. Shake remaining ingredients with cracked ice and strain into prepared glass. Add half a vanilla bean as a swizzle stick and a ribbon of lime peel. Serve on a glass plate with a tiny spoon to scoop out the fruit at the bottom of the drink. *Reproduced by kind permission of the Water Bar (www.tajhotels.com).*

WHITE ELEPHANT

Nuts for coconut? This drink is for you!

2 oz. coconut rum
1 oz. white crème de cacao
2 oz. cream of coconut
About 1 cup ice
Sweetened shredded coconut

Moisten the rim of a chilled parfait glass with crème de cacao. Dip glass in shredded coconut to coat rim. Blend remaining ingredients until smooth. Pour into prepared glass. Garnish with more coconut and white chocolate shavings. Or try it with toasted coconut.

INDEX

DRINKS BY PRIMARY ALCOHOLIC INGREDIENT

BOURBON

CACHAÇA

GIN

LIQUEURS

RUM

DRINKS BY FLAVOR

INTERNATIONAL HOT SPOTS

SIGNATURE DRINKS

SPECIALTY INGREDIENTS